Network and Information Systems (NIS) Regulations

A pocket guide for digital service providers

Network and Information Systems (NIS) Regulations

A pocket guide for digital service providers

ALAN CALDER

IT Governance Publishing

Every possible effort has been made to ensure that the information contained in this book is accurate at the time of going to press, and the publisher and the author cannot accept responsibility for any errors or omissions, however caused. Any opinions expressed in this book are those of the author, not the publisher. Websites identified are for reference only, not endorsement, and any website visits are at the reader's own risk. No responsibility for loss or damage occasioned to any person acting, or refraining from action, as a result of the material in this publication can be accepted by the publisher or the author.

Apart from any fair dealing for the purposes of research or private study, or criticism or review, as permitted under the Copyright, Designs and Patents Act 1988, this publication may only be reproduced, stored or transmitted, in any form, or by any means, with the prior permission in writing of the publisher or, in the case of reprographic reproduction, in accordance with the terms of licences issued by the Copyright Licensing Agency. Enquiries concerning reproduction outside those terms should be sent to the publisher at the following address:

IT Governance Publishing Ltd
Unit 3, Clive Court
Bartholomew's Walk
Cambridgeshire Business Park
Ely, Cambridgeshire
CB7 4EA
United Kingdom
www.itgovernancepublishing.co.uk

The author has asserted the rights of the author under the Copyright, Designs and Patents Act, 1988, to be identified as the author of this work.

First published in the United Kingdom in 2018 by IT Governance Publishing.

ISBN 978-1-78778-048-4

ABOUT THE AUTHOR

Alan Calder is the founder and executive chairman of IT Governance Ltd (*www.itgovernance.co.uk*), an information, advice and consultancy firm that helps company boards tackle IT governance, risk management, compliance and information security issues. Alan is an acknowledged international cyber security guru and a leading author on information security and IT governance issues. He has many years of senior management experience in the private and public sectors.

CONTENTS

INTRODUCTION

Technology has brought us into a world that many of us only poorly understand. While we may have some grasp of this technology, there is often a lack of real understanding as to how these technologies work and interact. A few decades ago, we understood that if the water levels fell then the hydroelectric plant would not be able to generate electricity. We knew that interchanges connected our phones to other phones elsewhere in the world. We had some appreciation of the fact that supermarkets and other retailers would have to call suppliers and wholesalers in order to have food delivered. Essential services and infrastructure were quite simple to understand.

Nowadays, so much has been automated and interlinked that it can be difficult to understand how our phone calls are connected or where our power comes from. Most people do not need to really understand how society continues to function. They do not need to know that RFID chips attached to crates of fruit make sure there is always fresh fruit on supermarket shelves. The electricity grid is driven by hundreds of power stations, with the flow managed, surpluses stored and shortfalls accounted for automatically. Our phones connect to remote cell towers and flicker between them to maintain the best possible connection. For the most part, as long as everything keeps working, we have no desire to understand any of this.

What we do want, however, is reassurance that these services will not be interrupted. This is not just for the benefit of the common person: our whole society relies on critical infrastructure, and this infrastructure is supported by a set of services. In the modern world, these services and infrastructure can be attacked not just physically but also digitally, and digital attacks can have significant repercussions in the physical world.

In 2014, a German steel factory suffered a cyber attack that caused significant physical damage to its machinery by turning off industrial controls.[1] More famously, the original Stuxnet worm infected the Natanz nuclear facility in Iran in 2010 and destroyed almost one fifth of the country's nuclear centrifuges.[2] In 2015, Ukraine was the victim of what is believed to be the first successful attack against a power grid, which left 230,000 people without power for up to six hours.[3]

Unfortunately, cyber criminals need to find just *one* weakness to infiltrate and potentially cause damage, but an organisation has to patch *all* of its vulnerabilities and defend against *all* types of attacks. These threats are significant not just because they are difficult to stop but also because they are increasingly within reach of even common criminals. Only a few years ago, a Polish teenager was able to hack into the Lodz tram network, derailing several carriages and injuring 12 people[4]; you might have reasonably assumed that such attacks came from state actors or well-funded terrorist or dissident groups, but it is the nature of

---

[1] SANS ICS, "German Steel Mill Cyber Attack", December 2014, *https://ics.sans.org/media/ICS-CPPE-case-Study-2-German-Steelworks_Facility.pdf*. For more information, see: Bundesamt für Sicherheit in der Informationstechnik, "APT-Angriff auf Industrieanlagen in Deutschland", *Die Lage der IT-Sicherheit in Deutschland 2014*, 2014, *www.bsi.bund.de/SharedDocs/Downloads/DE/BSI/Publikationen/Lage berichte/Lagebericht2014.pdf*.

[2] William J. Broad, John Markoff and David E. Sanger, "Israeli Test on Worm Called Crucial in Iran Nuclear Delay", *New York Times*, January 2011, *www.nytimes.com/2011/01/16/world/middleeast/16stuxnet.html*.

[3] Kim Zetter, "Inside the Cunning, Unprecedented Hack of Ukraine's Power Grid", *Wired*, March 2016, *www.wired.com/2016/03/inside-cunning-unprecedented-hack-ukraines-power-grid/*.

[4] John Leyden, "Polish teen derails tram after hacking train network", *The Register*, January 2008, *www.theregister.co.uk/2008/01/11/tram_hack/*.

information to be replicated and reused. As such, the threat is proliferating and will continue to do so.

In the European Union, threats to infrastructure and essential services can be especially severe because so many organisations operate across borders – a single service may be critical to several nations, so a single threat can affect all of them. This also means that each nation has an obligation to its neighbours to adequately protect its critical infrastructure and services.

These are the conditions of the modern world, and protecting our infrastructure and critical services is now recognised as essential. Without electricity, water, sewage, transport and the Internet, it is almost impossible to do business – or indeed for our modern society as a whole to function – and the EU is, after all, a major trading partnership.

The EU's Directive on security of network and information systems (NIS Directive)[5] is part of the legislated response to these threats.[6] It aims to establish a "high common level of security of network and information systems across the Union" (NIS Directive, Preamble), which will not only protect the Union's economy but also those of its trading partners, because they will benefit from the stability of the EU's infrastructure and services.

It is important to understand that the Directive is not just about cyber security or just about service continuity. It certainly requires cyber security and business continuity measures, but it is more accurately a synthesis of the two: cyber resilience. The fundamental thrust of the legislation is not simply that critical infrastructure organisations must be able to defend themselves, but that they must be able to continue functioning in the event of an incident. As part of this, there must also be a degree of

---

[5] Directive (EU) 2016/1148.

[6] Alongside legislation such as the General Data Protection Regulation (GDPR) and the ePrivacy Regulation.

communication and cooperation between EU Member States, both to share intelligence and to limit the spread of any attack.

Background

When the Directive was adopted in 2016, most EU Member States already had some regulations or laws regarding how critical infrastructure and services must be protected. These regulations and laws lacked a consistent approach, however: what one country thinks is an adequate level of cyber security may not meet their neighbour's standards, or while one country has applied conditions to a specific sector, their neighbour may not.

On the face of it, this may not appear to be a problem: a country's infrastructure should be its own concern, and it is in that country's interests to protect it, regardless of the measures its neighbours are taking or its antipathy to EU intervention. With such interconnected economies, however, and the prevalence of cross-border infrastructure and services, it is important for there to be some measure of consistency and cooperation between Member States. This is especially true of digital service providers (DSPs), which often operate across borders.

The EU, as most organisations should be aware, began and remains primarily a tool for streamlining business throughout the continent. To this end, it has largely focused on standardising and formalising trade and business. The EU has two types of legal instrument that are used to regulate business:

1. **Directives**
   These set minimum standards and parameters for the EU, but leave the actual implementation down to the states themselves. When a directive is passed, the EU sets a deadline by which every Member State must have put the directive into force, whether by law, regulation or other initiative.
2. **Regulations**
   These apply across the EU with the same authority as if they were local laws. Member States may choose to pass their own laws to implement a regulation (often because

the regulation requires each state to define some detail individually), but the regulation will apply regardless.

So, for any attempt to standardise practices across the Union, the EU can choose to either enforce a standard directly, or to set a minimum standard and rely on the Member States to determine more of the detail and, perhaps, to set their own standards higher. It is also worth noting that a regulation will generally set requirements intended to be applied by businesses, while directives will set conditions for states and state-run agencies.

The NIS Directive is, obviously, a directive, so each Member State will need to implement its own interpretation of the Directive's requirements. For the UK, these are 'The Network and Information Systems Regulations 2018 (NIS Regulations)', which were passed on 20 April 2018 and enforced on 10 May 2018.

Even though this approach can lead to some inconsistency, every Member State is, in theory, working from a common understanding – which is a major step up from having completely divorced systems. Having said that, organisations operating in multiple Member States need to be aware of possible differences in specific implementations – and that compliance with the NIS Regulations does not necessarily imply compliance outside the UK – although the 'common approach' is meant to prevent such situations. Regulations such as the EU's General Data Protection Regulation (GDPR), which attracted headlines in part because any journalist or blogger could write about it without waiting to see how the government intended to implement it, should not lead to any such inconsistencies.

A note on Brexit

While the UK will presumably be departing the EU in March 2019, the Regulations will continue to apply after that date, much like the GDPR. This should not be a surprise: the deadline for implementing the Directive was May 2018, when the UK was still a member of the EU. Furthermore, the UK has cemented both the GDPR and the NIS Directive into UK law and regulation through the Data Protection Act 2018 and the NIS

Regulations 2018, so it would be difficult (and foolish) to later renege on the commitment.

Other states have also been quick to implement the requirements of the Directive. In Germany, for instance, only minor amendments had to be made to the IT Security Act (IT-Sicherheitsgesetz) of 2015, which were completed in the Implementation Act (Umsetzungsgesetz) of June 2017,[7] while Slovakia has passed a law "on Cybersecurity and on Amendments and Supplements to certain Acts" (o kybernetickej bezpečnosti a o zmene a doplnení niektorých zákonov).[8]

Guidance

As mentioned earlier, the UK government transposed the NIS Directive into 'The Network and Information Systems Regulations 2018 (NIS Regulations)', which was passed on 20 April 2018. This content is supported by guidance from the European Union Agency for Network and Information Security (ENISA) and the UK's National Cyber Security Centre (NCSC) for DSPs and operators of essential services (OES) respectively.

Because of their typically cross-border offerings, the guidance in the NIS Directive itself is also of use for DSPs. For instance, Recital 48 explains that:

> Many businesses in the Union rely on digital service providers for the provision of their services. As some digital services could be an important resource for their users, including operators of essential services, and as such users might not always have alternatives available, this Directive should also apply to providers of such services.

---

[7] Bundesamt für Sicherheit in der Infomationstechnik, "Gesetz zur Umsetzung der NIS-Richtlinie", *www.bsi.bund.de/DE/DasBSI/NIS-Richtlinie/NIS_Richtlinie_node.html*.

[8] National Council of the Slovak Republic, "Act of January 30, 2018 on Cybersecurity and on Amendments and Supplements to certain Acts", January 2018, *www.nbusr.sk/en/cyber-security/index.html*.

It goes on to emphasise that:

> The security, continuity and reliability of the type of digital services referred to in this Directive are of the essence for the smooth functioning of many businesses. A disruption of such a digital service could prevent the provision of other services which rely on it and could thus have an impact on key economic and societal activities in the Union. Such digital services might therefore be of crucial importance for the smooth functioning of businesses that depend on them and, moreover, for the participation of such businesses in the internal market and cross-border trade across the Union.

The NIS Regulations further clarify the requirements for DSPs that fall under the UK's jurisdiction – that is, those that are either headquartered or have their representative in the UK. Additionally, the EU set out the security measures and incident reporting thresholds for DSPs in more detail in the European Commission's Implementing Regulation.[9]

The UK is taking two approaches to compliance – one for each of the types of organisation described in the Directive: DSPs and OES. This pocket guide focuses on the requirements for DSPs, while its partner will provide guidance for OES.

Key definitions

The following definitions are likely valuable to any organisation that needs to comply with the NIS Directive/Regulations. These definitions are shared between both pieces of legislation, so the risk of divergence from the original intent is diminished.

Network and information systems

   a) An electronic communications network – that is, "transmission systems and, where applicable, switching or routing equipment and other resources which permit the

---

[9] Commission Implementing Regulation (EU) 2018/151.[10] Directive 2002/21/EC, Article 2(a).

conveyance of signals by wire, by radio, by optical or by other electromagnetic means, including satellite networks, fixed (circuit- and packet-switched, including Internet) and mobile terrestrial networks, electricity cable systems, to the extent that they are used for the purpose of transmitting signals, networks used for radio and television broadcasting, and cable television networks, irrespective of the type of information conveyed"[10];

b) Any device or group of interconnected or related devices at least partially involved in automatic processing of digital data; or

c) Digital data stored, processed, retrieved or transmitted by one of the two elements above for their operation, use, protection and maintenance.[11]

Security of network and information systems

According to section 1(3)(g) of the NIS Regulations, this is "the ability of network and information systems to resist, at a given level of confidence, any action that compromises the availability, authenticity, integrity or confidentiality of stored or transmitted or processed data or the related services offered by, or accessible via, those network and information systems". The use of "at a given level of confidence" is particularly interesting, as it supports the notion that risk management practices are an essential element of compliance.

Incident

Under the NIS Regulations, this is "any event having an actual adverse effect on the security of network and information systems". Because it is a common term across a range of disciplines, however, it is valuable to also consider wider definitions:

---

[10] Directive 2002/21/EC, Article 2(a).

[11] Derived from NIS Directive, Article 4(1).

ISO/IEC 27000:2018 (ISO 27000, information security) provides the following definition for 'information security incident': "single or series of unwanted or unexpected information security events that have a significant probability of compromising business operations and threatening information security".

ISO 22301:2012 (ISO 22301, business continuity) provides the following definition for 'incident': "situation that might be, or could lead to, a disruption, loss, emergency or crisis".

ISO standards commonly distinguish between an event and an incident on the grounds that an 'event' is something that may or may not be an incident. ISO 27000, for instance, describes an 'information security event' as an "identified occurrence of a system, service or network state indicating a possible breach of information security policy or failure of controls, or a previously unknown situation that can be security relevant".

High common level of security

The Directive do not provide a definition for this, which leaves the actual 'level' up to negotiation between Member States. As it also aims for significantly increased cooperation across borders within the Union, the Directive will be driven by cooperation between competent authorities and computer security incident response teams (CSIRTs). This should result in a general coalescence around a set level of security in line with the priorities and objectives of businesses in the common market, and will doubtless be subject to some degree of change depending on the threats to infrastructure and the impact of the Directive on the ability to do business.

CHAPTER 1: SCOPE AND APPLICABILITY

Article 4(6) of the Directive specifies that DSPs are "any legal person that provides a digital service". A "digital service", in turn, is defined as "any service normally provided for remuneration, at a distance, by electronic means and at the individual request of a recipient of services".[12]

Unlike OES, governments aren't expected to identify DSPs – the Directive simply applies to all that provide any of the services that are categorised and listed in Annex III of the NIS Directive (section 1(2) of the NIS Regulations). However, the Information Commissioner's Office (ICO) – responsible for regulating UK DSPs – requires DSPs to identify themselves as such, and self-register by 1 November 2018.[13] That said, the government has stated that "If only part of a DSP's services are potentially within scope of the NIS Regulations, then the Government advises that the DSP contact the ICO (nis@ico.org.uk) to seek clarification on how the Regulations will apply".[14]

Online marketplaces

Online marketplaces provide a digital service that "allows consumers and traders to conclude online sales or service

---

[12] Directive (EU) 2015/1535, Article 1(b).

[13] ICO, "The Guide to NIS", *https://ico.org.uk/for-organisations/the-guide-to-nis/*.

[14] Department for Digital, Culture, Media & Sport, "Security of Network and Information Systems – Government response to targeted consultation on Digital Service Providers", August 2018, *https://assets.publishing.service.gov.uk/government/uploads/system/upl oads/attachment_data/file/737327/NIS_DSP_Consultation_Response_Final__1_.pdf*.

contracts with traders, and is the final destination for the conclusion of those contracts" (Recital 15).

This emphasis on being able to "conclude" their shopping is important, as the Recital goes on to explain that "It should not cover online services that serve only as an intermediary to third-party services through which a contract can ultimately be concluded. It should therefore not cover online services that compare the price of particular products or services from different traders, and then redirect the user to the preferred trader to purchase the product."

This is line with the government's targeted consultation on DSPs, which lists the following as *not* in scope[15]:

- Sites that redirect users to other services to make the final contract (e.g. price comparison sites).
- Sites that only connect buyers and sellers to trade with each other (e.g. classified advert sites).
- Sites that only sell directly to consumers on behalf of themselves (e.g. online retailers).

In its response to this consultation, the government emphasised that "the service has to be a genuine marketplace for goods or services and not an online retailer".[16] To further clarify, it stated that:

> Where a provider offers both retail services and online marketplace services, the online marketplace's services are covered by the NIS Directive. In relation to payment for those services, if a purchaser purchases a product from an

---

[15] Department for Digital, Culture, Media & Sport, "Security of Network and Information Systems – Targeted consultation on Digital Service Providers", March 2018,
https://assets.publishing.service.gov.uk/government/uploads/system/upl oads/attachment_data/file/694290/DSP_Targeted_Consultation__Fina l_.pdf.

[16] "Security of Network and Information Systems – Government response to targeted consultation on Digital Service Providers".

online marketplace, and payment for that product takes places through services provided by that online marketplace (whether third party or not) then they are within scope of the NIS Regulations. If the online marketplace transfers the purchases to the original product seller's website, and the purchase and transaction take place there, then they are not within scope of the NIS Regulations.

Finally, Recital 15 explains that "Computing services provided by the online marketplace may include processing of transactions, aggregations of data or profiling of users. Application stores, which operate as online stores enabling the digital distribution of applications or software programmes from third parties, are to be understood as being a type of online marketplace."

Online search engines

Online search engines provide a digital service that "allows the user to perform searches of, in principle, all websites on the basis of a query on any subject. It may alternatively be focused on websites in a particular language" (Recital 16).

The Recital goes on to explain that the Directive does "not cover search functions that are limited to the content of a specific website, irrespective of whether the search function is provided by an external search engine. Neither should it cover online services that compare the price of particular products or services from different traders, and then redirect the user to the preferred trader to purchase the product".

This is again in line with the government's targeted consultation, saying that if a site "offers search engine facilities [...] powered by another search engine, then the underlying search engine is required to meet the requirements of the NIS Directive".[17] It also

---

[17] "Security of Network and Information Systems – Targeted consultation on Digital Service Providers".

explicitly mentions that "Internal organisational search engines" are not in scope.

Cloud computing services

Cloud computing services provide a digital service allowing "access to a scalable and elastic pool of shareable computing resources. Those computing resources include resources such as networks, servers or other infrastructure, storage, applications and services" (Recital 17).

Recital 17 also provides the following definitions:

- Scalable: "computing resources that are flexibly allocated by the cloud service provider, irrespective of the geographical location of the resources, in order to handle fluctuations in demand".
- Elastic pool: "those computing resources that are provisioned and released according to demand in order to rapidly increase and decrease resources available depending on workload".
- Shareable: "those computing resources that are provided to multiple users who share a common access to the service, but where the processing is carried out separately for each user, although the service is provided from the same electronic equipment".

For further clarification, the government's response explained that:

Cloud services are limited to those that are scalable and elastic - by which we mean computing resources that are flexibly allocated by the cloud service provider, irrespective of the geographical location of the resources, in order to handle fluctuations in demand (scalable) and computing resources that are provisioned and released according to demand in order to rapidly increase and decrease resources available depending on workload (elastic).[18]

The government's targeted consultation lists the following Cloud services as those "primarily (but not exclusively)" considered DSPs:

- Infrastructure as a Service (IaaS): "the delivery of virtualised computing resource as a service across a network connection, specifically hardware – or computing infrastructure – delivered as a service".
- Platform as a Service (PaaS): "services that provide developers with environments on which they can build applications that are delivered over the internet, often through a web browser".
- Software as a Service (SaaS): "provided the resources available to the customer through that software are changeable in an elastic and scalable way. The Government considers that this would likely exclude most current online gaming, entertainment or Voice over Internet Protocol (VOIP) services, as the resources available to the user are not scalable, but may include services such as email or online storage providers, where the resources are scalable".

Self-identification

Recital 57 states that "Member States should not identify digital service providers, as this Directive should apply to all digital service providers within its scope. [...] This should enable digital service providers to be treated in a uniform way across the Union". However, as stated earlier, the ICO has stated that DSPs within scope should register by 1 November 2018.

The reason the Directive does not require Member States to explicitly identify DSPs lies in the fact that it is intended to apply to DSPs across the Union without exception or variance. This

---

[18] "Security of Network and Information Systems – Government response to targeted consultation on Digital Service Providers".

ensures that DSPs can expect equal treatment wherever they operate, streamlining business and providing a guaranteed minimum level of reliability for organisations and consumers across the EU. This is quite different from how OES are treated, for which the NIS Directive simply provides a set of parameters, letting individual Member States determine how these apply within local law.

Some special cases

Recital 53 and Article 16(11) of the Directive specify that micro and small enterprises do not fall under the scope of the Directive. Section 1(3)(e)(ii) of the NIS Regulations identifies these in line with the European Commission's definitions as DSPs that employ fewer than 50 people and whose annual turnover and/or annual balance sheet total does not exceed €10 million.[19]

Some organisations established outside the Union may also be designated DSPs and bound by the Directive's requirements. In line with Recital 65, if "it is apparent that the digital service provider is offering services to persons in one or more Member States", then the organisation should designate a representative within the Union, so it will fall under the jurisdiction of that Member State. This representative will be designated in writing to act on the DSP's behalf in relation to the Directive, so will need to be available to any relevant CSIRTs and competent authorities. Likewise, if a DSP is based within a Member State, but offers services outside of that state, its competent authority is still responsible for overseeing those cross-border activities within the EU.

---

[19] Micro and small enterprises are defined by the European Commission in 2003/361/EC, which states that "a small enterprise is defined as an enterprise which employs fewer than 50 persons and whose annual turnover and/or annual balance sheet total does not exceed EUR 10 million", and that "a microenterprise is defined as an enterprise which employs fewer than 10 persons and whose annual turnover and/or annual balance sheet total does not exceed EUR 2 million".

It may be difficult to enforce the Directive on DSPs based outside the EU, but it is nonetheless an important point. OES will essentially be limited to using the services of DSPs that comply with the Directive. In addition, common consumers and other organisations will also want the reassurance that the services they are using and investing in are actually reliable.

Operators of essential services

Although this pocket guide focuses on DSPs, the NIS Directive also imposes requirements on OES. These are stricter than those imposed on DSPs – particularly from a supervisory point of view – because of the higher risk OES typically face.

It is entirely possible for an organisation to provide services both as a DSP and as an OES, but for other organisations it may be less clear whether they are one or the other. In the UK, the NIS Regulations specify in Section 8(3) that competent authorities are permitted to designate some edge case OES before 10 November 2018. This can only happen if three conditions are met:

1. The OES meets the sector, subsector and essential service requirements.
2. The service provided relies on network and information systems.
3. An incident has the potential to significantly disrupt the provision of the essential service.

Although there are rules governing OES across borders, there are no rules for DSPs that operate across borders. This is because, as previously noted, DSPs should be treated uniformly across the Union, so a single DSP should have a good understanding of the conditions and be able to provide its services throughout the EU, regardless of where it is based.

CHAPTER 2: AUTHORITIES AND BODIES

As well as requiring Member States to set "security and notification requirements for operators of essential services and for digital service providers", the NIS Directive also specifies that they must "designate national competent authorities, single points of contact and CSIRTs with tasks related to the security of network and information systems".[20]

Each of these bodies will play an important role in how the Directive is applied in the Member States and across the EU. In the UK, the NCSC will operate as the CSIRT and the single point of contact, and as a technical authority on cyber security. Competent authorities have been determined on a sectoral basis for OES in the UK, but DSPs have been assigned just one competent authority: the ICO, which is also responsible for regulating GDPR compliance in the UK.

Competent authorities

Competent authorities are the organisations or agencies that oversee compliance with laws and regulations implemented on the basis of the NIS Directive. There is no specified limit on the number of competent authorities a Member State can set and several countries – other than the UK – have already decided to assign them on a sectoral or regional basis. However, others have opted to appoint just one competent authority.

Although the NCSC and competent authorities like the ICO are meant to oversee compliance, the Directive states that they should have "no general obligation to supervise digital service providers" and should "only take action when provided with evidence […] that a digital service provider is not complying with the requirements of this Directive, in particular following the occurrence of an incident" (Recital 60).

---

[20] NIS Directive, Article 1.

These relatively lenient requirements apply to DSPs only – not OES. Recital 49 offers some insight:

> In practice, the degree of risk for operators of essential services […] is higher than for digital service providers. Therefore, the security requirements for digital service providers should be lighter. Digital service providers should remain free to take measures they consider appropriate to manage the risks posed to the security of their network and information systems.

Regardless of their level of involvement, the primary question that each Member State will need to answer is 'What makes a competent authority competent?'. Recital 30 of the Directive offers some guidance:

> In view of the differences in national governance structures and in order to safeguard already existing sectoral arrangements or Union supervisory and regulatory bodies, and to avoid duplication, Member States should be able to designate more than one national competent authority responsible for fulfilling the tasks linked to the security of the network and information systems of operators of essential services and digital service providers under this Directive.

As does Recital 61:

> Competent authorities should have the necessary means to perform their duties, including powers to obtain sufficient information in order to assess the level of security of network and information systems.

Essentially, competent authorities should be able to both assess how organisations apply the principles and enforce them. Some authorities will doubtless be provided with additional funding or resources, and whole new agencies may be necessary for some sectors. The NIS Regulations provide specific powers for competent authorities in the UK to inspect DSPs and OES, as well as enforcement powers.

While competent authorities are regulators, the Directive makes it clear that cooperation, rather than dictatorial assertiveness, is key to making sure it is effective. Recital 31 states:

> As this Directive aims to improve the functioning of the internal market by creating trust and confidence, Member State bodies need to be able to cooperate effectively with economic actors and to be structured accordingly.

Fundamentally, the competent authorities should operate to facilitate business where possible, rather than to repress it. 'Cooperation' is a common theme throughout the Directive, and leads into the requirements for cooperation across the EU.

CSIRTs

The NIS Directive requires each Member State to establish a CSIRT. CSIRTs already exist in a number of countries, the most famous team almost certainly being the first – the CERT Division – which was established at Carnegie Mellon University in the US and helped to create US-CERT. In the UK, the CSIRT is the NCSC.

CSIRTs are specialist units charged with providing guidance and support in the event of a significant incident, and tracking incidents globally so that useful information can be shared and lessons can be learned. In relation to the NIS Directive, this means the CSIRT must be able to react appropriately to incidents that could have significant consequences for critical infrastructure, so that their impact can be minimised. Such units will conduct research into current and evolving threats, maintain an intelligence function to identify sources of threats, keep track of vulnerabilities and suitable mitigations, and define good-practice frameworks to protect infrastructure.

A number of CSIRTs already in existence across the EU will see increases in their authority and the tools at their disposal by being established in law. As ENISA states in relation to formal, official support for the role: "an officially recognised mandate is one of the very first steps for a successful national CSIRT."[21]

The Directive states that each Member State's CSIRT should be "adequately equipped, in terms of both technical and organisational capabilities, to prevent, detect, respond to and mitigate network and information system incidents and risks" (Recital 34). Because they will act as a central resource for all DSPs and OES, the level of investment and authority they are given will be essential to the Directive's success.

All CSIRTs across the EU will be part of the CSIRTs network, which is intended to "contribute to the development of confidence and trust between the Member States and to promote swift and effective operational cooperation" (Article 12). Functionally, it will be an information-sharing arrangement with a mandate to ensure that common threats can be dealt with through coordinated action. There are, of course, limitations on the information that can be shared, as most CSIRTs will be in some way related to national security.

Single points of contact

The single point of contact is each Member State's coordinating function for the NIS Directive. This involves coordinating the different authorities within the Member State (i.e. CSIRTs and competent authorities) as well as across the EU. The single point of contact will also receive annual reports on incidents from competent authorities and CSIRTs.

The NCSC is the UK's single point of contact, meaning that it will "act as the contact point for engagement with EU partners on [network and information systems], coordinating requests for action or information and submitting annual incident

---

[21] ENISA, "NIS Directive and national CSIRTs", February 2016, *www.enisa.europa.eu/publications/nis-directive-and-national-csirts*.

statistics."[22] If a Member State chooses to appoint only one competent authority, that body will also automatically act as the single point of contact.

Where the CSIRTs are involved in the CSIRTs network, the single point of contact will represent the Member State in the Cooperation Group described below.

Cooperation Group

The NIS Directive has established a Cooperation Group, which operates at a high level. It comprises the single points of contact from each Member State, the EU Commission and ENISA. This is effectively an EU-wide governing function for protecting critical infrastructure, and has several important duties:

- Providing strategic guidance for the CSIRTs network.
- Developing best-practice methods for exchanging information relating to incidents.
- Evaluating national strategies on the security of network and information systems.
- Coordinating information exchange with other EU institutions and offices.
- Discussing standards and specifications relevant to the NIS Directive.
- Exchanging best practice on a range of topics and practices relevant to securing critical infrastructure.

Critically, the Cooperation Group will work with the Commission to produce implementing regulations that will apply across the EU, such as the Implementing Regulation of 30 January 2018, which further specified requirements for DSPs under the Directive. Although implementing regulations will be limited in their frequency, this is clearly an influential position critical to the ongoing security of the European Union.

---

[22] NCSC, "Introduction to the NIS Directive", January 2018, *www.ncsc.gov.uk/guidance/introduction-nis-directive*.

Powers and penalties

Within each Member State, different agencies and bodies will have differing powers to enforce the local requirements. In the UK, competent authorities are able to grant extensions to incident reports, which reflects the government's position that "implementing the requirements of the Directive will be realistic and will take into account the circumstances of each sector as appropriate".[23]

In addition to this, competent authorities will be able to impose penalties and other regulatory actions on their relevant sector much as the ICO can for transgressions of the GDPR.

The NIS Regulations have introduced the following range of penalties:

- A maximum of £1 million for "any contravention [of the Regulations] which the enforcement authority determines could not cause a NIS incident".
- A maximum of £3.4 million for "a material contravention which the enforcement authority determines has caused, or could case, an incident resulting in a reduction of service provision […] for a significant period of time".
- A maximum of £8.5 million for "a material contravention which the enforcement authority determines has caused, or could case, an incident resulting in a disruption of service provision […] for a significant period of time".
- A maximum of £17 million for "a material contravention which the enforcement authority determines has caused, or could cause, an incident resulting in an immediate threat

---

[23] Department for Digital, Culture, Media & Sport, "Security of Network and Information Systems: Government response to public consultation", August 2017, *www.gov.uk/government/uploads/system/uploads/attachment_data/file/636207/NIS_Directive_-_Public_Consultation__1_.pdf*.

to life or significant adverse impact on the United Kingdom economy".

Although the maximum fine is high, the UK government has provided assurances that DSPs and OES should not be fined under both the NIS Regulations and the GDPR for the same incident unless there is "reason for them to be penalised under different regimes for the same event because the penalties might relate to different aspects of the wrongdoing and different impacts".[24]

The level of fine is not fixed across the EU, so other Member States may set higher or lower levels as they see fit. The Netherlands intends to set a maximum fine of €5 million for non-compliance,[25] while Slovakia has varying fines depending on the organisation's total annual turnover for the "previous accounting year", though these will not exceed €300,000, or €600,000 for repeated violations.[26]

---

[24] "Security of Network and Information Systems: Government response to public consultation".

[25] Rijksoverheid, "Regels ter implementatie van richtlijn (EU) 2016/1148 (Cybersecuritywet)", February 2018, *www.rijksoverheid.nl/binaries/rijksoverheid/documenten/brieven/2018/02/07/tk-wvst-cybersecuritywet-nib-richtlijn-versie-rvs/tk-wvst-cybersecuritywet-nib-richtlijn-versie-rvs.pdf*.

[26] Act of January 30, 2018 on Cybersecurity and on Amendments and Supplements to certain Acts.

CHAPTER 3: COMPLYING WITH THE DIRECTIVE

As described earlier, the NIS Directive is not a piece of legislation that applies directly to organisations – although the NIS Regulations do – so speaking of the 'Directive's requirements' is slightly misleading. It is not that the Directive tells organisations how to operate within the market; rather, it tells Member States to legislate within a set of parameters. Having said that, understanding what the Directive actually demands of Member States – and what the relevant competent authorities have said on the matter – can be illuminating.

For OES in the UK, compliance with the NIS Regulations – and, by extension, the Directive – is achieved by meeting requirements set by the NCSC and relevant competent authorities. However, as previously noted, the risk for DSPs is lower than for OES, and, as such, their security requirements are lighter. Article 16 of the Directive provides some detail on the two main requirements facing DSPs:

1. Minimum security measures; and
2. Mandatory incident notification.

Minimum security measures

Article 16(1) states the following:

> [DSPs must] identify and take appropriate and proportionate technical and organisational measures to manage the risks posed to the security of network and information systems which they use in the context of offering services […] Having regard to the state of the art, those security measures shall ensure a level of security of network and information systems appropriate to the risk posed, and shall take into account the following elements:
>
> (a) the security of systems and facilities;
> (b) incident handling;
> (c) business continuity management;

(d) monitoring, auditing and testing;

(e) compliance with international standards.

The NIS Regulations mention all five elements in Section 12(2)(c) as things for DSPs' measures to "take into account". That requirement also refers to Article 2 of the Implementing Regulation, which goes into more detail for each of these elements, stipulating what sub-elements DSPs need to consider. That article also notes that DSPs need to keep "adequate documentation" so they can demonstrate compliance to the ICO and stakeholders.

In addition, ENISA has published its "Technical Guidelines for the implementation of minimum security measures for Digital Service Providers", designed to help Member States and DSPs provide "a common approach" when it comes to the required security measures.[27] The Guidelines list 27 security objectives, including security measures that take the 5 elements listed above into account. This means that meeting these 27 objectives can also support compliance with the security requirements of the NIS Regulations and Directive. The Guidelines also recognise that different organisations need different levels of maturity depending on their specific circumstances: each objective can be achieved at three different 'sophistication levels', in accordance with the results of a risk assessment that identifies the organisation's particular needs.

Regardless of how much note your organisation takes of ENISA's guidance, it should remember that there are two keys to applying security measures:

1. Most importantly, they must be "appropriate to the risk" (Article 16(1) of the NIS Directive; Section 12(2)(a) of the NIS Regulations).
2. Consider both technical and organisational approaches.

---

[27] ENISA, "Technical Guidelines for the implementation of minimum security measures for Digital Service Providers", February 2017, *www.enisa.europa.eu/publications/minimum-security-measures-for-digital-service-providers*.

Appropriate to the risk

Ultimately, DSPs are free to judge their own adequate measures, as long as they are appropriate to the risk. Taking a risk-based approach lies at the heart of cyber security best practice; it is, after all, critical to fully understand a threat in order to treat it both adequately and proportionately. Without useful intelligence about the threats you face, it is difficult to make sure you are spending the right money on the right measures.

Taking a risk-based approach means having to establish the risks that your organisation faces or is likely to face at an early stage in your compliance project. You should also determine your organisation's risk appetite (or risk tolerance), if you have not done so already.

For the purposes of compliance, you do not have to seek out every single risk your organisation may face. The Directive and Regulations focus on risks that could affect IT continuity, so it would be sensible to look for relevant sources of guidance on information security risk management, such as international standards (as suggested by the laws themselves). However, whether or not you choose to follow best-practice guidance, there are several methodologies an organisation can apply in assessing and managing its risks, which generally fall into two schools:

1. **Asset-based assessments**
    An asset-based risk assessment examines the threats to the organisation's assets, and determines the vulnerabilities that those threats might exploit. A vulnerability without a threat cannot be exploited and, therefore, is not a risk. Equally, a threat with no vulnerability to exploit is not a risk.

2. **Scenario-based assessments**
    Scenario-based risk assessments examine the consequences of an event more generally. For instance, what harm is likely to come to the organisation if there were an earthquake? What about a break-in?

Each method has benefits and drawbacks, and the organisation should consider which is most appropriate to its needs. After establishing all risks – regardless of the approach – you should decide what measures to take. There are generally four types of response:

1. **Avoid** – terminating the source of the threat, perhaps by ending a business activity or changing the way it is done.
2. **Modify** – implementing security controls to reduce the impact and/or likelihood of the risk.
3. **Share** – transferring (part of) the risk to another party, such as through insurance.
4. **Retain** – actively choosing to tolerate the risk.

Naturally, retaining the risk is only appropriate in specific circumstances. There are typically four reasons:

1. The risk is within the organisation's risk appetite – in other words, the risk is within a pre-defined acceptable range;

2. Mitigating the residual risk would cost too much considering its potential harm – in other words, implementing measures would be *inappropriate* for the level of risk;

3. It is not feasible to avoid the risk – the activity subject to the risk is essential to the organisation or irreplaceable; or

4. To pursue an opportunity, as some risks can be pursued for potential positive impacts and retained on that basis. For instance, an organisation may wish to move into a volatile market, which could result in significant gains.

You should also bear in mind that 'actual' measures, whether they consist of modifying or sharing the risk, do not have to eliminate the risk altogether – they can simply be enough to lower the risk to within acceptable boundaries (determined by your risk appetite). Ultimately, it is a matter of balancing the cost of treating a risk (taking potential legal costs into account) against the impact of that risk.

Technical and organisational measures

The measures you apply to mitigate risks need to consider both technical and organisational approaches. After all, people have to implement and/or operate technology, and follow defined processes. For instance, the first security objective outlined in ENISA's Technical Guidelines –establishing and maintaining an information security policy – is clearly an organisational measure. The ninth objective – establishing and maintaining appropriate security measures to ensure the security of supporting utilities (e.g. electricity or fuel) – has both technical and organisational aspects. Ensuring the security of such utilities may entail putting a policy – an organisational measure – in place, but also putting physical and/or technical controls in place, such as standby power generators.

All 27 security objectives are explained and mapped to ISO/IEC 27001:2013's reference controls in the *Appendix 1*.

Mandatory incident notification

Article 16(3) of the Directive says the following on incident notification:

> [DSPs must] notify the competent authority or the CSIRT without undue delay of any incident having a substantial impact on the provision of a service [...] that they offer within the Union. Notifications shall include information to enable the competent authority or the CSIRT to determine the significance of any cross-border impact.

This is in line with the NIS Regulations, which state in Section 12(3):

> [DSPs] must notify the Information Commissioner about any incident having a substantial impact on the provision of any of the digital services [...] that it provides.

Article 1 of the Implementing Regulation makes clear that the DSP itself is responsible for assessing the scale of an incident, its geographical spread and the significance of damages to service users in the EU – not any of the supervisory bodies.

Article 4(1) defines the thresholds for what constitutes a "substantial impact".

The metrics that determine whether an incident is of "substantial impact" are:

- Service unavailability for more than 5 million user hours in the Union;
- The loss of confidentiality, integrity, availability or authenticity of data accessed over networks or information systems, affecting more than 100,000 users in the Union;
- The incident creates a risk to public safety, public security or loss of life; or
- The material damage to at least one user in the Union exceeds €1 million.

If any of these are the case, the DSP is required to notify the ICO within 72 hours of becoming aware of the incident. More generally speaking, competent authorities should also "be informed about potential new risks", and should encourage DSPs to "voluntarily report any incident whose characteristics have been previously unknown to them such as new exploits, attack-vectors or threat actor, vulnerabilities and hazards" (Recital 11 of the Implementing Regulation).

After notifying the competent authority or CSIRT, DSPs may further notify other authorities or CSIRTS of the incident, should it indeed have a significant impact across borders. By their nature, DSPs are likely to be used remotely – users are not bound to the Member State where the DSP is based. ENISA has provided a figure that explains the overall incident notification process for DSPs at EU level, which is reproduced in *Figure 1*[28].

---

[28] ENISA, "NIS Directive and national CSIRTs", February 2016, *www.enisa.europa.eu/publications/nis-directive-and-national-csirts*.

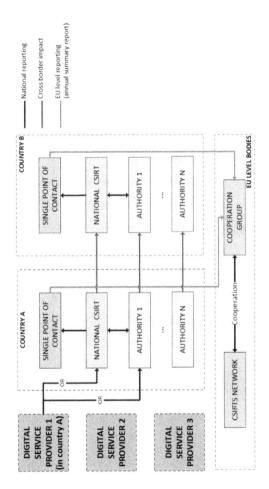

Figure 1: Incident notification process for DSPs at EU level

In essence, the DSP is responsible for reporting incidents to either the CSIRT or the relevant competent authority, which will inform the other body. The CSIRT and competent authority then share information with the single point of contact – referred to as 'national reporting' – assuming that the competent authority does not also act as the single point of contact.

If there is a cross-border impact, the CSIRT and competent authority will report it to their respective bodies in the affected Member State(s). The CSIRT and competent authority in that/those Member State(s) will then communicate with one another, and report the incident to their single point of contact. Regardless of the cross-border impact, the single point(s) of contact will inform the Cooperation Group of the incident, which will cooperate with the CSIRTs network. This ensures that CSIRTs across the EU have the best possible information about incidents and can respond appropriately.

Earlier on, we explained that, because of the lighter security requirements for DSPs compared to OES, competent authorities have no need to supervise DSPs unless provided with evidence that the DSP in question is not complying with the Directive's requirements. Naturally, the most obvious evidence would be when an incident of "substantial impact" occurs – competent authorities would then need to investigate whether the organisation was compliant at the time. The lack of immediate supervision could result in DSPs forgetting to keep or even generate evidence that they do comply. This stresses the importance of not only achieving and maintaining compliance, but also ensuring you can prove it. The lighter requirements do not imply lighter penalties.

International standards

The NIS Regulations, NIS Directive and Implementing Regulation all note that the required security measures can be managed under the guidance of existing international standards (Section 12(c)(v) of the NIS Regulations; Article 16(1e) of the NIS Directive; Article 2(5) of the Implementing Regulation).

However, none of them provide any specifics on how to go about implementing them.

If your organisation opts for a standards-based approach, it must consider a lot of variables, including which standards to select, which parts of your organisation will be in scope, and whether to seek certification against any or all of the chosen standards.

Some of our recommended choices to help DSPs manage information security risks effectively include:

- ISO/IEC 27001:2013 (ISO 27001), *Information technology — Security techniques —Information security management systems — Requirements*;

- ISO/IEC 27002:2013 (ISO 27002), *Information technology — Security techniques — Code of practice for information security controls*;

- ISO/IEC 27035:2016 (ISO 27035), *Information technology — Security techniques —Information security incident management*; and

- ISO 22301:2012 (ISO 22301), *Societal security — Business continuity management systems — Requirements*.

There are also standards that provide guidance specifically for Cloud services, which we discuss in more detail later in this pocket guide.

All these standards take the required risk-based approach, and ISO 27001, ISO 27002 and ISO 27035 are also regularly referred to in the guidance that the NCSC has provided for UK OES.[29]

As mentioned earlier, Article 2(6) of the Implementing Regulation is explicit about the fact that DSPs must have "adequate documentation available" so the relevant competent authority can "verify compliance with the security elements". In

---

[29] NCSC, "Table view of principles and related guidance", July 2018, *www.ncsc.gov.uk/guidance/table-view-principles-and-related-guidance*

order to meet that requirement, you should make sure that process flows produce evidence of compliance as a natural by-product. For instance, if you have a process for confirming that critical software is up to date and fully patched, it should produce a record that demonstrates this. The cumulative records of this process will, over time, demonstrate good practice. Having an ISO 27001-aligned information security management system (ISMS) in place would also produce evidence of good practice and ensure that security is maintained. Such an approach would be favourably looked upon by regulators.

CHAPTER 4: IMPLEMENTING CYBER RESILIENCE

Cyber resilience is a blend of cyber security, incident response and business continuity. An effective cyber resilience framework can protect an organisation from the majority of attacks and incidents, while also maximising its durability when an incident does occur. The principle behind cyber resilience is that an organisation can do a great deal to prevent incidents or mitigate their impact, but incidents remain inevitable. This is one good reason for the Implementing Regulation to mandate business continuity, which defines it as "the capability of an organisation to maintain or as appropriate restore the delivery of services at acceptable predefined levels following a disruptive incident" (Article 3).

As the technology to commit cyber crime becomes more accessible and the number of vulnerabilities that any organisation might be subject to increases, cyber attacks become more certain. This assumption is supported by statistics: according to a 2018 UK government survey,[30] 43% of all UK businesses had suffered at least one breach or cyber attack in the previous 12 months, which was higher among medium-sized (64%) and large firms (72%) – and this is despite a significant increase in cyber security investment.

For organisations that do suffer an incident, such as a cyber attack, it is critical that they have processes in place to respond to the incident, reduce its impact and quickly recover to business as usual. This requires a comprehensive framework that considers people, processes and technology – people, after all, are critical to security and to ensuring that processes and technologies are applied correctly and consistently, which is, of

---

[30] Department for Digital, Culture, Media & Sport, "Cyber Security Breaches Survey 2018", April 2018, *www.gov.uk/government/statistics/cyber-security-breaches-survey-2018*.

course, why the Directive requires both technical and organisational measures.

Common principles across various cyber resilience frameworks include that the project must be led from the top of the organisation, and must be capable of continually adapting to new threats and changing environments. These are characteristics of any successful, ongoing business project, and cyber resilience should be treated in much the same way.

Your organisation could develop a cyber resilience capability by simply going through the guidance and references provided by one of these frameworks, but this is likely to result in an inconsistent and disorganised set of processes without a larger appreciation for how they fit into the organisation. A successful project must take a more considered, holistic approach.

ISO standards – especially ISO 27001 (information security) and ISO 22301 (business continuity) – provide specifications for management systems that can be integrated to provide an effective framework for cyber resilience, incorporating further guidance from standards such as ISO 27002 and ISO 27035.

However, helpful as these standards may be, they are not designed for compliance with the NIS Directive, NIS Regulations, Implementing Regulation or any other piece of legislation. Rather, they are intended to provide **guidance** on good practice to protect information and information systems (the ISO 27000 family), and help organisations survive and quickly recover from incidents (ISO 22301). As such, any organisation using these standards to any degree still needs to ensure that it has taken all steps necessary to achieve, maintain and prove compliance with the law.

ISO 27001 and ISO 27002

ISO 27001 is the international standard for information security management, and provides a structured approach to protecting an organisation's information assets. Meanwhile, ISO 27002 – the 'code of practice' – provides comprehensive implementation guidance that builds on ISO 27001.

Like other ISO management system standards, ISO 27001 recognises that there are a number of core functions that any management system must rely upon and builds onto them. This makes information security part of the way the organisation operates, rather than simply being a side concern. This also takes the organisation's business environment and obligations into account, ensuring that the ISMS is relevant to the organisation.

The first step to ensure top management commitment: the organisation must both direct and support the ISMS from the very top, which might be the board or senior management, and includes taking accountability for the success of the project. This ensures that the ISMS can be operated in line with the organisation's wider business objectives while providing evidence that information security is a topic to be taken very seriously. It also ensures that the ISMS meets all of the requirements your organisation may face.

ISO 27001 advocates taking a risk management approach to information security, in line with Recital 44 of the Directive:

> A culture of risk management, involving risk assessment and the implementation of security measures appropriate to the risks faced, should be promoted and developed through appropriate regulatory requirements and voluntary industry practices.

In other words, the organisation should decide how to mitigate its risk on the basis of an informed assessment – that is, based on the risks it actually faces.

Once again, this exists within a larger framework that takes the organisation's business environment into account. ISO 27001's risk management process is kept deliberately open to allow the organisation to use whatever methodology is already familiar or appropriate to the business. Rather than prescribing a method in detail, it simply sets out a more general process that can be adopted by most existing risk management methodologies.

Clause 6.1 of ISO 27001 requires the organisation's risk assessment process to:

- Define both risk acceptance criteria and criteria for conducting a risk assessment;
- Produce "consistent, valid and comparable results";
- Identify risks associated with the loss of confidentiality, integrity and availability of information assets;
- Analyse each risk to identify the likelihood of it occurring and the potential impact if it does occur; and
- Evaluate the risks against the organisation's risk acceptance criteria to decide upon appropriate responses.

The output of a risk assessment will be a risk treatment plan that describes how the organisation will treat the risks it has identified. For the most part, this will involve applying controls. Such controls can fulfil a range of functions, but they generally fall into one of three categories:

1. **Preventive**
   Preventive controls are intended to prevent risks from occurring or to reduce their likelihood. For instance, a rigorous patching programme reduces the amount of time that applications are vulnerable to exploitation, which in turn reduces the likelihood that an attacker will be able to take advantage of them.

2. **Detective**
   Detective controls identify events and incidents, allowing the organisation to take steps to prevent an incident from occurring, gather forensic evidence for later action or react to reduce the impact of an incident. For instance, an intrusion detection system (IDS) identifies anomalous activity that could be an intrusion into the organisation's networks. This activity may not be an actual intrusion, but it could be symptomatic of a vulnerability that the organisation can then act to resolve.

3. **Reactive**
   Reactive controls come into play when an event or incident occurs and seek to reduce their impact. For instance, a process that isolates a network segment can prevent an attacker from exfiltrating data, progressing further into the system or identifying further weaknesses to exploit.

It is, of course, possible for a control to fulfil several functions – a CCTV camera might discourage a criminal from breaking into an office (preventive), identify when a break in occurs (detective) and provide evidence of the intruder's identity (reactive). Meanwhile, a firewall is primarily preventive, as it tries to keep intruders out, but could also function as a detective control, notifying the user of suspicious activity.

As previously mentioned, it is important to understand that the organisation should select controls on the basis of the actual risks it faces, and should balance the cost of treating a risk against the impact of the risk. As part of this, the organisation should be sure that it understands the 'hidden' costs of an incident, including reputational damage, legal harm, and fines and regulatory action. Annex A of ISO 27001 provides a reference set of controls that are generally applicable and supported by guidance in ISO 27002, but organisations are free to draw their controls from any source or design their own.

There is a great deal more that could be said on the topic of risk assessment. For more information, we recommend that you read *Information Security Risk Management for ISO27001/ISO27002*.[31]

The controls to directly manage risks are supported by a range of management procedures that tie information security into 'ordinary' business processes. These include communication, competence and staff awareness, which ensure that the ISMS is well understood, and the organisation has the skills and knowledge to implement and maintain it.

The ISMS must also be assessed to make sure that it is functioning correctly and is in line with the documented processes. This is achieved through a combination of ongoing, regular measurements and internal audits. The results of these

---

[31] Alan Calder and Steve Watkins, "Information Security Risk Management for ISO27001/ISO27002", April 2010, www.itgovernance.co.uk/shop/product/information-security-risk-management-for-iso27001iso27002.

assessments are then reviewed by management so that any discrepancies or anomalies can be resolved. Just as management must initiate and support the ISMS, it is also responsible for ensuring its continuing efficacy. This set of processes allows the organisation to continually improve its ISMS, which ensures it remains effective over time and in the face of changing technologies and environments.

Another key component of an ISO 27001-conforming ISMS, and possibly part of this set of processes, is penetration testing – systematic and controlled probing for vulnerabilities in your applications and networks. Regular penetration testing is the most effective way of identifying exploitable vulnerabilities in your infrastructure, allowing appropriate mitigation to be applied. It would also be good practice to test any new services or networks before making them available. Vulnerabilities are discovered and exploited all the time by opportunistic criminal hackers who use automated scans to identify targets. Closing these security gaps and fixing vulnerabilities as soon as they become known are essential steps to keeping your networks and information systems safe and secure.

Standards for Cloud services

There are a few standards specifically aimed at Cloud services:

- **ISO/IEC 27017:2015**[32]
  ISO 27017 is the *Code of practice for information security controls based on ISO/IEC 27002 for cloud services*. ISO 27002 provides expanded guidance on the Annex A controls in ISO 27001; ISO 27017 expands this content to make the guidance more applicable to Cloud service providers.

---

[32] Available at: *www.itgovernance.co.uk/shop/product/iso-27017-2015-information-security-controls-for-cloud-services*.

- **ISO/IEC 27036-4:2016**[33]
  ISO 27036-4, *Guidelines for security of cloud services*, is intended for both Cloud service customers and providers.

- **The Cloud Security Alliance Cloud Controls Matrix (CSA CCM)**[34]
  The CSA CMM provides a controls framework that is "specifically designed to provide fundamental security principles to guide cloud vendors and to assist prospective cloud customers in assessing the overall security risk of a cloud provider", and is available online for free. It is also regularly referred to in ENISA's Technical Guidelines.

ISO 27017 emphasises a few points. For instance, an organisation's security policy for its information assets should stretch to its Cloud computing policy. By that principle, the provider should also "agree and document an appropriate allocation of information security roles and responsibilities with its cloud service customers, its cloud service providers, and its suppliers" (Clause 6.1.1). The same clause explains:

> Data and files on the cloud service provider's systems that are created or modified during the use of the cloud service can be critical to the secure operation, recovery and continuity of the service. The ownership of all assets, and the parties who have responsibilities for operations associated with these assets, such as backup and recovery operations, should be defined and documented. Otherwise, there is a risk that the cloud service provider assumes that the cloud service customer performs these vital tasks (or vice versa), and a loss of data can occur.

ISO 27017 continues to make similar points, such as the advice that any assets stored in the Cloud must be recorded in an

---

[33] Available at: www.itgovernance.co.uk/shop/product/isoiec-27036-4-2016-iso27036-4-standard-cloud-security-guidelines.

[34] Cloud Security Alliance, "Cloud Controls Matrix Working Group", March 2017, https://cloudsecurityalliance.org/group/cloud-controls-matrix.

inventory. Ultimately, the overall message of the Standard is that Cloud providers have to take comparable measures to any other type of service providers – thus the similarity to ISO 27002. Cloud providers should take note of the fact that their assets are not in 'traditional' digital or paper formats only; they face a slightly different set of risks and may need to take extra precautions.

Clause 5.2 of ISO 27036 explains in more depth how the risk to Cloud-based assets differ from more traditional ones:

> Cloud service customers have limited control over the location, access, processing and protection of information placed in the cloud service. Additionally, cloud service customers may not be made aware of incidents, breaches, failures or other issues affecting the service in a timely manner. The limited control, coupled with a lack of information about the cloud service performance and security, presents a major risk of using the cloud service. When making an acquisition decision, the cloud service customer will need to evaluate these risks in relation to the information to be placed in the cloud and the dependence of the business on the information and the cloud service.

The Standard lists the typical threats and risks that Cloud services may face, which is followed by suggested adjustments to a more general risk assessment and related processes. ISO 27036 also provides information on controls that may be suitable for Cloud providers, but the Standard's list is not nearly as comprehensive as the CSA CCM.

Where both ISO 27017 and ISO 27036 focus mainly on practices and are a bit more general (in line with the ISO 27000 family), the Matrix is much more specific to the technologies typically used by Cloud providers. As a control set, the CSA CCM also tends to integrate well with ISO 27001, which provides the specifications for a management system without being too precise about which controls an organisation might use.

ISO 22301

Many of the same processes used in information security management apply to a business continuity management system (BCMS) aligned to ISO 22301 – in particular, the more general management processes, such as ensuring management oversight and review, communication, awareness, competence and documentation management. This means that they can be applied simultaneously to integrate both management systems. For instance, the same process used to make staff aware of the organisation's need for information security can also be used to express the importance of continuity. Because these processes are shared, the organisation can save time and money by integrating these management systems together.

A BCMS that conforms to ISO 22301 provides a well-defined incident response structure, ensuring that when an incident occurs, responses are escalated in a timely manner and the right people take the right actions to respond effectively. As Article 2(3) of the Implementing Regulation points out: "Business continuity management […] means the capability of an organisation to maintain or as appropriate restore the delivery of services at acceptable predefined levels following a disruptive incident". The key elements involved in a BCMS are business impact analysis (BIA), risk assessment and the business continuity plan (BCP).

BIA is the process of identifying the harm that could come to the organisation if a given business function is disrupted. It also takes into account how that harm changes over time. After all, some incidents will have a very small or negligible impact unless they persist, while other incidents have an immediate impact that does not change over time.

This information becomes the basis for prioritising each business process for recovery in event of a disruptive incident. ISO 22301's approach to risk assessment focuses on risks to "the organization's prioritized activities and the processes, systems, information, people, assets, outsource partners and other resources that support them".[35] Treatment of these risks should be in line with both the organisation's continuity objectives and its risk appetite.

By combining the assessed threat that each risk poses to the organisation's critical services, the organisation is able to prioritise its responses. These priorities inform the BCP(s).

The BCP is critical to the BCMS: it describes how the organisation will respond to disruptions, in both general and specific terms. For instance, it should include contact details for authorities and key suppliers, and sources of support that can be called on during disruptions, while also setting out the detailed steps involved in responding to and recovering from incidents that affect the organisation's critical services.

The BCP relies on being tested regularly – in line with Article 2(3) of the Implementing Regulation, which points out that any established plans must be "assessed and tested on a regular basis for example, through exercises". Without testing, there is little way of knowing whether the plan is effective. Additionally, there is no real way to improve the plan, which, by extension, means that the organisation cannot improve its ability to respond to and recover from disruptive incidents.

Although it would, of course, be good business practice to implement a BCMS that covered the entire organisation, for the purposes of NIS Directive compliance, only the network will be in scope, so achieving certification to ISO 22301 might not be necessary. However, certification can give you a competitive advantage and lead to new contractual opportunities. It could also help your organisation comply with other legislation, and generally protect your organisation from harm.

ISO 27035

ISO 27035 outlines concepts, phases and overall guidelines for information security incident management, and can be easily

---

[35] ISO 22301:2012, Clause 8.2.3 a).

implemented by organisations also aiming to meet ISO 27001's requirements, as many of the two standards' processes line up. ISO 27035's structured approach to incident response consists of five phases:

1. Plan and prepare
2. Detection and reporting
3. Assessment and decision
4. Responses
5. Lessons learnt

The first phase, detailed in Clause 5.2 of the Standard, focuses on the more general management processes, such as ensuring management oversight and review, communication, awareness, competence and documentation management.

The second phase becomes more specific for information security incident management, which is dedicated to internally reporting potential incidents as soon as possible after any unusual activity has been detected.

The third phase, assessment and decision, looks into assessing the situation and deciding whether the event classifies as an 'information security incident'. If so, the incident has to be contained, information has to be collected to pinpoint what exactly happened, and a log has to be kept, which can be analysed at a later stage.

In the fourth phase, responses, any agreed incident management activities have to be carried out after tasks and responsibilities have been assigned. Such activities could include reviewing any reports made and logs kept, reassessing the damage and notifying the relevant people or bodies. This point is particularly relevant for the Directive's purpose, as any incident of substantial impact has to be reported.

Finally, after all urgent action has been taken, the whole situation and process can be reviewed, including any existing management systems, plans or procedures, and notes can be taken on how the incident could have been mitigated or even prevented. The most important part of "lessons learnt" is ensuring that potential improvements are actually implemented.

Combining standards

With an ISO 27001-aligned ISMS in place and integrated with an ISO 22301-aligned BCMS, taking note of incident response procedures as guided by ISO 27035, an organisation has a systematic approach to cyber resilience and compliance with relevant laws and regulations, including the NIS Regulations, NIS Directive and Implementing Regulation. For more detailed guidance, DSPs can take further note of ISO 27002 and, if relevant, any or all of the Cloud standards.

Because these management systems operate on a process of continual improvement, they can adapt to changes in the legal environment and evolving threats. This is critical: an organisation that cannot continue to defend itself from cyber attack and other incidents will inevitably suffer, and regulators will see this and act accordingly. Cyber resilience is an ongoing concern that should adapt and grow as an organisation does, not a project to be completed once and left to stagnate.

APPENDIX: MAPPING OF ENISA'S TECHNICAL GUIDELINES AND ISO 27001 ANNEX A

Security objective	Description	ISO 27001 Annex A reference controls
1: Information security policy	Establish and maintain an information security policy.	A.5 Information security policies
2: Risk management	Establish and maintain an appropriate governance and risk management framework to identify and address risks.	All
3: Security roles	Assign security roles and responsibilities to designated staff.	A.6.1 Internal organization
4: Third-party management	Establish and maintain a policy that sets out the security requirements for customer and supplier contracts.	A.15.1 Information security in supplier relationships
5: Background checks	Perform background checks before hiring new personnel	A.7.1 Prior to employment
6: Security knowledge and training	Ensure relevant staff have the knowledge to perform security-related tasks adequately, and provide regular training.	A.6.1.1 Information security roles and responsibilities A.7.2.2 Information security awareness, education and training

7: Personnel changes	Establish and maintain a process for managing staff changes.	A.7.3.1 Termination or change of employment responsibilities
8: Physical and environmental security	Implement controls, and establish and maintain policies for the physical and environmental security of data centres.	A.11 Physical and environmental security
9: Security of supporting utilities	Implement security measures for supporting utilities.	A.11.2.2 Supporting utilities
10: Access control to network and information systems	Implement measures, and establish and maintain policies for access to business resources.	A.6.1.2 Segregation of duties A.6.2.2 Teleworking A.9.2.1 User registration and de-registration A.9.2.2 User access provisioning A.9.2.4 Management of secret authentication information of users A.9.3.1 Use of secret authentication information A.9.4.1 Information access restriction A.9.4.2 Secure log-on procedures A.9.4.3 Password management system A.9.4.4 Use of privileged utility programs A.11.1.1 Physical security

		perimeter A.11.1.2 Physical entry controls A.11.1.4 Protecting against external and environmental threats A.11.1.6 Delivery and loading areas A.11.2.3 Cabling security A.13.1.1 Network controls A.13.1.3 Segregation in networks A.13.2.1 Information transfer policies and procedures
11: Integrity of network components and information systems	Take steps to prevent security incidents, thus maintaining the integrity of networks, platforms and services.	A.13.1 Network security management
12: Operating procedures	Establish and maintain procedures for operating key network and information systems.	A.12.1.1 Documented operating procedures A.12.5.1 Installation of software on operational systems A.13.2.1 Information transfer policies and procedures A.14.2.2 System change control procedures

13: Change management	Establish and maintain change management procedures for key network and information systems.	A.12.1.2 Change management A.12.5.1 Installation of software on operational systems A.12.6.2 Restrictions on software installation A.14.2.2 System change control procedures A.14.2.3 Technical review of applications after operating platform changes A.14.2.4 Restrictions on changes to software packages
14: Asset management	Implement configuration controls, and establish and maintain asset management procedures for key network and information systems.	A.6.1.1 Information security roles and responsibilities A.8.1.1 Inventory of assets A.8.1.2 Ownership of assets A.8.2.1 Classification of information A.13.2.1 Information transfer policies and procedures
15: Security incident detection and response	Establish and maintain procedures for detecting and responding to security incidents effectively. Incorporate a	A.16.1.5 Response to information security incidents

	process for learning from past experiences.	
16: Security incident reporting	Establish and maintain incident reporting and communication procedures.	A.16.1.5 Response to information security incidents
17: Business continuity	Prepare contingency plans and a continuity strategy to ensure service availability.	A.17.1 Information security continuity
18: Disaster recovery capabilities	Prepare a disaster recovery capability in the case of natural and/or major disasters.	A.16.1.1 Responsibilities and procedures A.17.1.1 Planning information security continuity A.17.1.2 Implementing information security continuity
19: Monitoring and logging	Establish and maintain procedures and/or systems for monitoring and logging activity.	A.12.4 Logging and monitoring
20: System tests	Establish and maintain procedures for regularly testing key network and information systems.	A.14.2 Security in development and support processes
21: Security assessments	Establish and maintain procedures for performing security assessments of critical assets.	A.12.6.1 Management of technical vulnerabilities A.18.2.2 Compliance with security policies and standards

22: Compliance	Establish and maintain a policy to check internal policies against relevant legal requirements, and against industry best practice and standards.	A.18 Compliance
23: Security of data at rest	Implement mechanisms to adequately protect data at rest.	A.6.1.2 Segregation of duties A.7.1.1 Screening A.7.1.2 Terms and conditions of employment A.7.3.1 Termination or change of employment responsibilities A.8.2.2 Labelling of information A.8.2.3 Handling of assets A.9.1.1 Access control policy A.9.1.2 Access to networks and network services A.9.2.3 Management of privileged access rights A.9.4.1 Information access restriction A.9.4.4 Use of privileged utility programs A.9.4.5 Access control to program source code A.12.1.4 Separation of development, testing and

		operational environments A.12.2.1 Controls against malware A.12.5.1 Installation of software on operational systems A.13.1.1 Network controls A.13.1.3 Segregation in networks A.13.2.1 Information transfer policies and procedures A.13.2.3 Electronic messaging A.13.2.4 Confidentiality or nondisclosure agreements A.14.1.2 Securing application services on public networks A.14.1.3 Protecting application services transactions
24: Interface security	Establish and maintain a policy for securing the interfaces of services that process personal data.	None
25: Software security	Establish and maintain a policy for ensuring that developed software respects security.	None

26: Interoperability and portability	Ensure customers can interface with other digital services and/or migrate to another provider offering a similar service. (Cloud computing services and online marketplaces only.)	None
27: Customer monitoring and log access	Grant customers access to relevant transaction and performance logs. (Cloud computing services only.)	A.12.4.1 Event logging A.12.4.2 Protection of log information A.12.4.3 Administrator and operator logs A.12.4.4 Clock synchronisation

FURTHER READING

IT Governance Publishing (ITGP) is the world's leading publisher for governance and compliance. Our industry-leading pocket guides, books, training resources and toolkits are written by real-world practitioners and thought leaders. They are used globally by audiences of all levels, from students to C-suite executives.

Our high-quality publications cover all IT governance, risk and compliance frameworks and are available in a range of formats. This ensures our customers can access the information they need in the way they need it.

For more information on ITGP and branded publishing services, and to view our full list of publications, visit *www.itgovernancepublishing.co.uk*.

To receive regular updates from ITGP, including information on new publications in your area(s) of interest, sign up for our newsletter at *www.itgovernancepublishing.co.uk/topic/newsletter*.

Branded publishing

Through our branded publishing service, you can customise ITGP publications with your company's branding.

Find out more at *www.itgovernancepublishing.co.uk/topic/branded-publishing-services*.

Related services

ITGP is part of GRC International Group, which offers a comprehensive range of complementary products and services to help organisations meet their objectives.

For a full range of resources on the NIS Regulations, please visit *www.itgovernance.co.uk/nis-directive*.

Training services

The IT Governance training programme is built on our extensive practical experience designing and implementing management systems based on ISO standards, best practice and regulations.

Our courses help attendees develop practical skills and comply with contractual and regulatory requirements. They also support career development via recognised qualifications.

Learn more about our training courses and view the full course catalogue at *www.itgovernance.co.uk/training*.

Professional services and consultancy

We are a leading global consultancy of IT governance, risk management and compliance solutions. We advise businesses around the world on their most critical issues and present cost-saving and risk-reducing solutions based on international best practice and frameworks.

We offer a wide range of delivery methods to suit all budgets, timescales and preferred project approaches.

Find out how our consultancy services can help your organisation at *www.itgovernance.co.uk/consulting*.

Industry news

Want to stay up to date with the latest developments and resources in the IT governance and compliance market? Subscribe to our Daily Sentinel newsletter and we will send you mobile-friendly emails with fresh news and features about your preferred areas of interest, as well as unmissable offers and free resources to help you successfully start your projects. *www.itgovernance.co.uk/daily-sentinel*.

EU for product safety is Stephen Evans, The Mill Enterprise Hub, Stagreenan, Drogheda, Co. Louth, A92 CD3D, Ireland. (servicecentre@itgovernance.eu)

www.ingramcontent.com/pod-product-compliance
Lightning Source LLC
Chambersburg PA
CBHW070857070326
40690CB00009B/1879